Which toad has zapped the fly?

a   b   c

1

What does this person need to do his job? Circle the object.

2

3

Circle the one that doesn't belong.

Where in the world is this building?

4

Draw a line to
connect the pairs
of pirates.

5

What is missing
from this guitar?

6

Draw the picture in the grid, copying square by square.

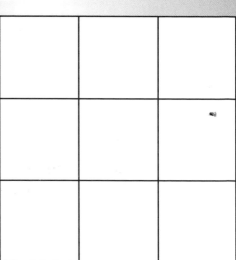

Color this picture.

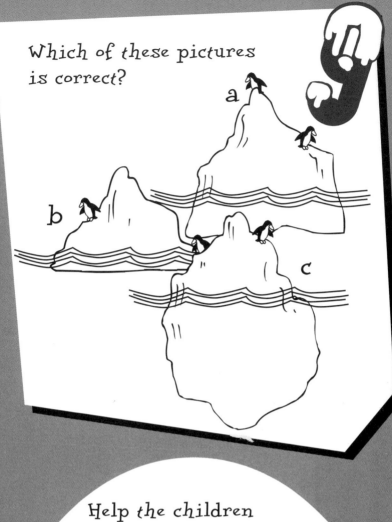

Which of these pictures is correct?

a

b

c

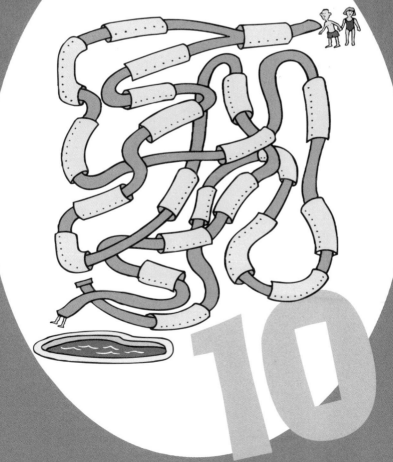

Help the children through the water tubes.

11 Color the sections marked with a dot to reveal a bouncy creature.

12 Help the bunny through the maze to his carrot.

One piece is missing from this puzzle. Can you see which one it is?

13

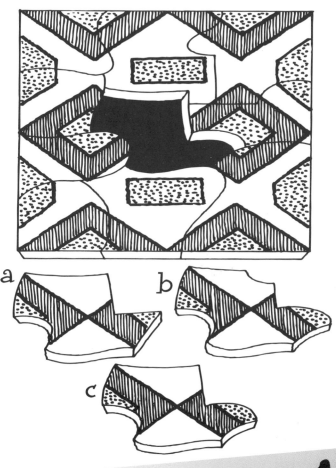

a

b

c

How many differences can you find between these pictures?

14

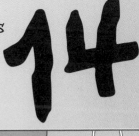

15

S	N	E	A	K	E	R	S
J	D	I	N	Z	P	W	O
W	L	O	F	U	N	K	C
F	I	B	Y	T	C	A	K
W	O	L	J	E	A	N	S
E	N	J	K	L	P	R	T
K	N	U	Y	V	G	I	O
C	S	H	I	R	T	E	B
K	L	R	V	O	P	J	G

Find these boys' clothes by reading across and down in the grid.

16

How many words can you think of that rhyme with "rain"? Write them on the cloud.

My first is in wood, not in food.
My second is in dam, not in dim.
My third is in look, not in hook.
My fourth is in rain, not in pain.
My fifth is in dump, not in damp.
My last is in laser, not in later.

17

18

Can you spot the mistakes
in this picture?

19

Starting with number 1, connect the dots to complete the picture.

20

How many different shapes can you count in this picture?

Complete these
slow math problems.

21

6 + 3 = 9

2 + 2 = 4

5 + 4 = 9

22

Color this picture
by following the
number-color
key.

1 = red
2 = green
3 = yellow
4 = blue
5 = purple

23

Follow the different paths to see where each of the bears lives.

24

Which of these pictures doesn't belong and why?

25

Use the picture clues to fill in the word trail. The last letter of each word is the first letter of the next.

26

Write these times on the lines.

9:55

8:40

2:30

27

Change "cow" to "rug" by changing one letter on every line.

cow

_____

_____

_____

rug

28

Which is the missing piece of this puzzle?

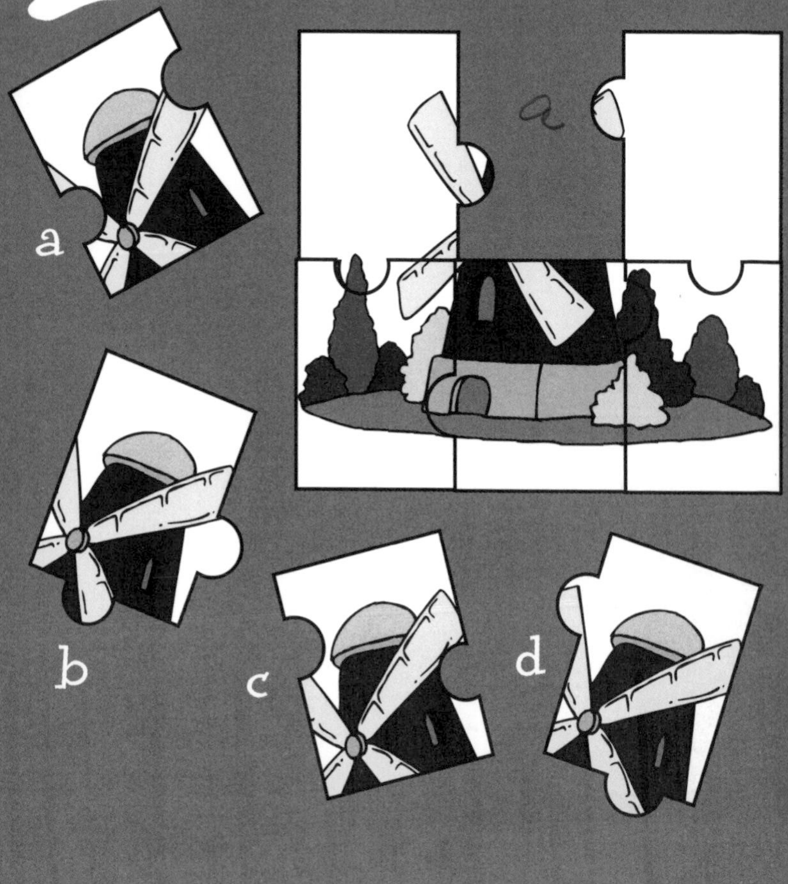

a

b

c

d

Follow the lines to see which child is going to the beach.

29

a

b

c

Draw a line from the number problems to the correct answers.

30

21 ÷ 7

3 × 4

6 − 2

4

3

12

32

Name as many
animals as you can
that have scales.

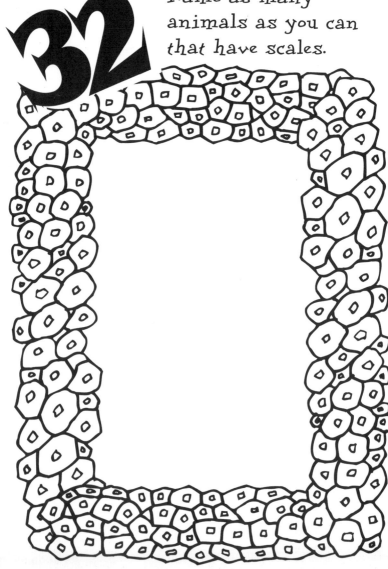

Circle the things that are wrong in this picture.

33

RODEO

Look at the pairs of pictures. Put a check in the box by the one that is heavier.

34

35

Circle the one that doesn't belong.

36

What does this person need to do his job? Look at the shelf and write the answer on the line.

_____

Which roadrunner wins the race? The highest number wins.

Can you figure out what has gotten stuck in the chimney?

40 What do giant pandas eat? Write your answer in the box.

Starting at number 1, follow the dots to complete the picture.

41

Which is the biggest mammal in the world?

42

43

Which *two* pumpkins are exactly the same?

a

b

c

d

44

The words and pictures are mixed up. Draw lines to link the labels with the correct pictures.

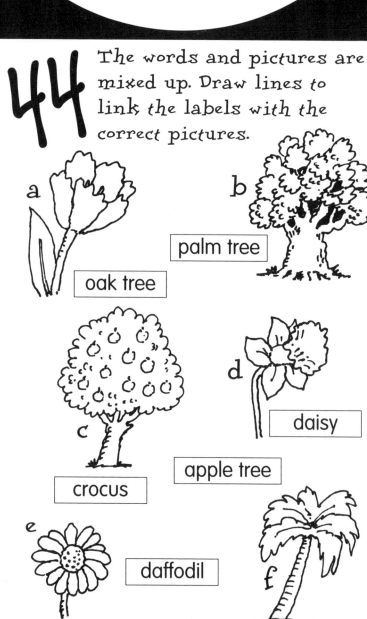

a

b

palm tree

oak tree

c

d

daisy

crocus

apple tree

e

daffodil

f

45

How many bubbles has Billy blown? Write your answer on the line.

23

How many coconuts can you count? 10

46

How many words can you think of beginning with K? Write them on the knight's banner.

47

48

Look carefully at these two pictures. Can you spot the differences between them?

Shade in the areas marked with a dot to reveal the hidden picture.

Who doesn't belong in outer space?

51

How many sides do four squares have altogether?

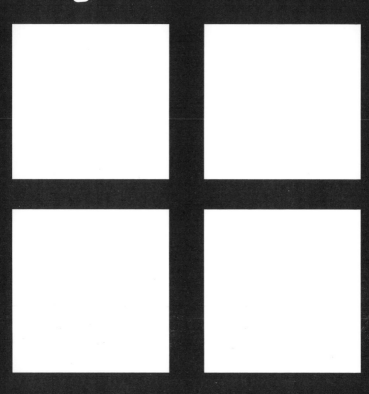

52

Starting at number 1, connect the dots to complete the picture.

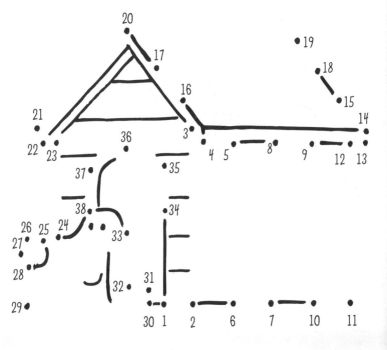

Draw hands and a face on this clock to show the time when you wake up!

Help the ghost hunters find the ghosts.

55

Help the rabbit find his way out of the vegetable patch.

56

Starting with the letter "y", cross out every other letter to find out which sport Mark likes best.

y f c o u o i t p b k a h l d l j

Football

Color *this* jungle picture. **57**

Fill in the missing numbers. **58**

| 2 | 4 | 6 | 8 | 10 | 12 | 14 | 16 | 18 |

| 5 | 10 | 15 | 20 | 25 | 30 | 35 | 40 |

| 10 | 20 | 30 | 40 | 50 | 60 | 70 |

59 Look in the word search grid for the names of eight buildings. Circle the words.

```
Q W C H U R C H L
T J B O D V D X I
O S Z U A F B J G
W C P S K J A R H
E H V E S E R C T
R O X R B H N T H
C O T T A G E O O
J L A M L H T D U
D K T V V N U G S
W L R C A S T L E
```

60 Count the pieces of pepperoni on the pizza.

10

How many new words
can you make from the
words "striped umbrella"?

61

Help the wizard sort out
these silhouettes. Draw a
circle around each toad.

62

63 Can you spot the mistakes in this picture?

64 Help the alien through the maze to the mothership.

Write the times
on the lines.

65

3:00

9:15

1:30

Which animals are
mixed up here? Write
them on the lines.

66

_____

_____

_____

_____

67 Draw lines to match the people with their jobs.

a

l + 1 =

b

ᵃ gardener

c

ᶜ doctor

ᵇ teacher

68 Do you know what the five senses are?

Shade in *the* areas marked
with a dot *to* reveal *the*
hidden picture.

Write *the* first letter of each picture
in *the* center of *the* puzzle wheel.
The letters will spell
a month of *the* year.

71

How many dinosaur spots are there altogether?

72

Help the squirrel through the maze.

Unscramble the letters on Sam the soccer player's shirt to find out which team he plays for.

73

SHOUTNO
MONDAY
_____
_____

How many books can you count in the bookcase? 35

74

75

Two of these frogs are identical. Can you spot them?

a

b

c

d

e

f

76

Help the knight find his way to the castle.

If each line is worth five minutes of burning time, how long will each candle last?

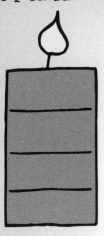

_____ minutes

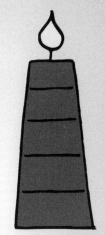

_____ minutes

_____ minutes

_____ minutes

Fill in the missing numbers to complete these number patterns.

78

9, 18, _27_ **, 36,** _45_ **, 54**

_4_ **, 8,** _12_ **,** _16_ **, 20,** _24_

30, _25_ **, 20,** _15_ **,** _10_ **, 5**

Cross out the letters that appear twice in the grid. The letters that remain will spell a fruit.

P	B	S	L	E
W	F	A	M	K
M	J	O	J	G
C	O	G	F	W
K	L	B	S	H

Look carefully at these two pictures. Can you spot the differences between them?

Guide the pilot through the clouds to the airport.

Find these pets by reading across and down in the word search grid.

Y	H	U	I	O	P	B	L
S	A	F	G	H	J	U	K
R	M	O	U	S	E	D	S
C	S	O	L	H	J	G	A
A	T	V	B	N	M	I	C
T	E	C	A	F	Y	E	H
E	R	A	B	B	I	T	Y
G	O	L	D	F	I	S	H
D	O	G	E	O	H	A	M

83

Unscramble the names of these Major League soccer teams.

HOCIGAC RIEF

Chicago ~~Change~~ Fire

WEN KORY ERD LUBSL

New York Red Bulls

AL LAGYXA

_____

HIPALAIDHELP ONNIU

_____

84

Where in the world would you find this animal?

Measure these skyscrapers. **85**

| 10 units | 8 units | 7 units |

86

Draw lines to match
the objects with the
silhouettes.

a
b
c
d
e

1
2
5
3
4

 Can you fill in the missing numbers?

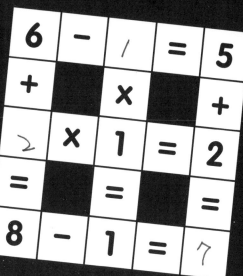

6	−	1	=	5
+		×		+
2	×	1	=	2
=		=		=
8	−	1	=	7

88

Follow the lines to find out who has the banana.

Count the groups of stars and planets. Put a check in the box if there is an even number and an ✗ if there is an odd number.

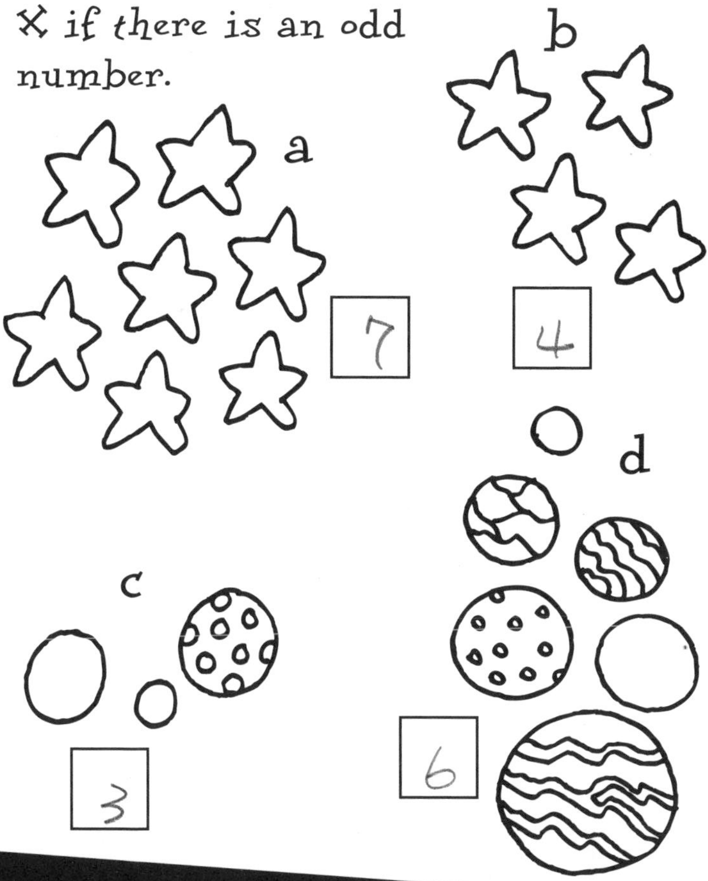

a

7

b

4

c

3

d

6

Unscramble these letters to find out who lives in this cave.

Z I D W A R

91

Use the pictures as clues to complete the crossword.

¹b x c t i n g
²s a
l
i
n
³j a v e l i n
⁴g o l f

92

Draw a circle around the percussion instruments.

a

b

c

d

e

Can you solve this riddle?

I have six letters. I am a building.
My first is in cat but not in bat.
My second is in man but not in men.
My third is in sail but not in tail.
My fourth is in salt but not in sale.
My fifth is in low but not in cow.
My sixth is in sea but not in sat.

I am a

_____

Use the pictures as clues to complete the crossword.

1 across

1 down

1. s h i p
   a
2. D i n g h y
   l
3. r o w b o a t
   o
   a
   t

95

Draw the picture in the grid, copying square by square.

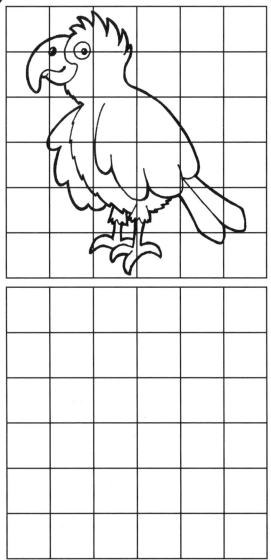

96

A diplodocus was a type of what?

a) transportation
b) dinosaur
c) bird

Each symbol represents a different number of minutes. Add them up to see who wins the race. The lowest number wins!

a b c

🍦 1

☺ 2

🐝 3

FINISH

Can you find the word PUPPY six times in this grid?

R Y W Y T O P P S
P U P P Y S U V N
U D A P U P P Y F
P K L U E S P P Q
P V B P H E Y P U
Y A P U P T S J K
U A E P U P P Y H
P D U P N E T R E
S D T Y L E J V C
W P U E S P F Q P

99 Starting at number 1, connect the dots to complete the picture.

100 Starting with the letter L, cross out every other letter. You will end up with the name of a famous landmark.

L E G I H F I F

W E T L O T M

O K W S E G R

_____

How many buttons
can you count? 12

101

Help the caveman
to his cave by
spelling the name
of an animal.

102

S K O
   Q   I
U
   S   L
      F
B   H
   P
E   A
   C   F

103 Work out how many goals were scored in each match. Which team scored the most goals?

A. PRETEND MADRID 1 - ASTON VANILLA 3

B. TOPSBOROUGH 4 - SPARS 0

C. OLDCASTLE 5 - WEST SPAM 1

D. ASTON VANILLA 3 - PRETEND MADRID 4

E. SPARS 3 - TOPSBOROUGH 1

F. WEST SPAM 2 - OLDCASTLE 2

104 Circle the one that doesn't belong.

Write the first letter of
each picture in the center
of the puzzle wheel.
The letters will spell a boy's name.

Follow the lines to
connect each kite to
a number. Draw the
correct number of bows
on the strings.

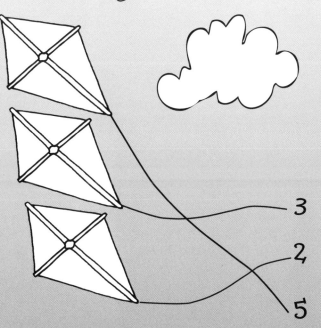

3

2

5

107

Do you know which sport Jonathan is about to play?

_____

108

Help Sid through the maze to the ice-cream sundaes.

How many wild animals can you find hiding in the jungle? Circle each one as you find it.

109

Two of these houses are the same. Can you match the pair?

110

a

b

c

d

e

f

g

h

111

Shade in the areas marked with a dot to reveal the hidden picture.

112

Draw straight lines from the problems to the answers.

2 x 2

10 + 5

9 ÷ 3

2 x 4

8

3

15

4

Cross out the letters that
appear twice in the grid.
The letters that remain
will spell the name of a pet.

M	H	P	A	O
D	N	E	S	I
R	C	J	M	D
I	E	J	P	N
H	S	R	O	T

Write the first letter
of each picture clue
in the boxes to make
words.

P	E	t

y	O	g

r	E	d

115

Unscramble these cities.

AIRPS — Paris

DOOLNN — London

SOL NGAEELS — los angeles

EDYSNY — Sydney

116

Write all the math problems you can think of with six as the answer.

= 6

Look in the word search grid for the names of five planets. Circle them as you find them.

117

```
E W Q T P R Y U
Z X C V S B N M
M E R C U R Y A
E A W D T F A R
B R A E F I O S
C T S A T U R N
V H Q S G V M A
L P N O O T S R
U T A V E N U S
```

Write the first letter of each picture in the center of the puzzle wheel. What do the letters spell?

118

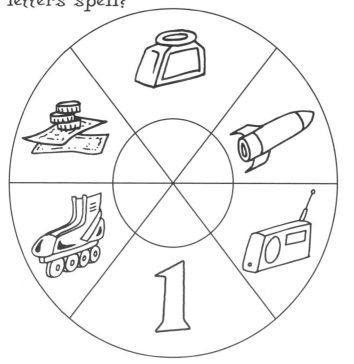

119

Color this picture.

120

Draw lines to connect the footprints with their owners.

a   b   c   d

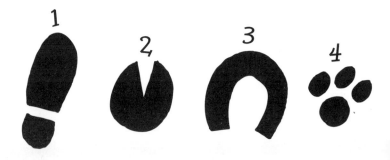

1   2   3   4

Use the pictures as clues to complete the crossword.

	¹K										
²r	a	b	b	i	t		⁴f	l	e	a	
	n						r				
	³g	r	a	s	s	h	o	p	p	e	r
	a						g				
	r										
	o										
	o										

Draw lines to connect the words in the left column to the words in the boxes to make five new words.

BREAK   SOME

HAND   BELL

EAR   HORSE

BLUE   RING

SEA   FAST

123

These ten balls make a triangle shape. Move only three balls to make the triangle face the other way.

124

Shade in the areas marked with a dot to reveal the hidden picture.

125

Unscramble the letters in the dinosaur's spots to find out his name.

126

Draw lines to match the pairs.

127

Color this picture.

128

Follow the numbered stepping stones from 1-5 to help Scott cross the river to his friends.

Can you help the spy work out the secret message?

THE PLANS ARE HIDDEN.

What vehicle has this snake eaten?

131

Do you know which came first?

132

Connect the balloons to the number line.

6

13

20

16

0   5   10   15   20

How many new words can you make from "CLUMSY CAMEL"?

Cross out the letters that appear twice. Unscramble the remaining letters to find a word.

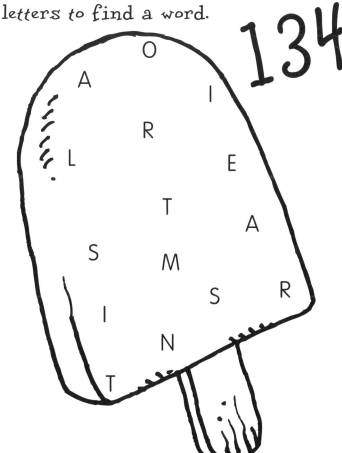

135 Count the windows in this skyscraper. How many floors are there?

136 Do the math by counting the tiny stars on each cupcake.

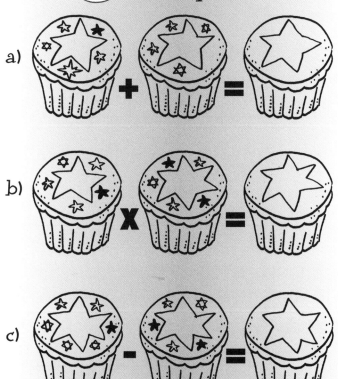

a)

b)

c)

Circle the one
that's different.

Using the fruit code,
do the math and write
the answers in the boxes.

banana = 4	pineapple = 2	pear = 3

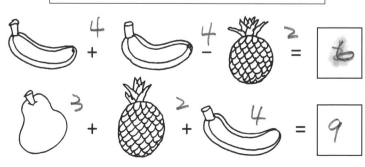

$4 + 4 - 2 = \boxed{6}$

$3 + 2 + 4 = \boxed{9}$

Draw the picture in the grid, copying square by square.

140

Follow the lines to discover which pirate finds the treasure.

a b c d

d

Which comet has the longest tail? **141**

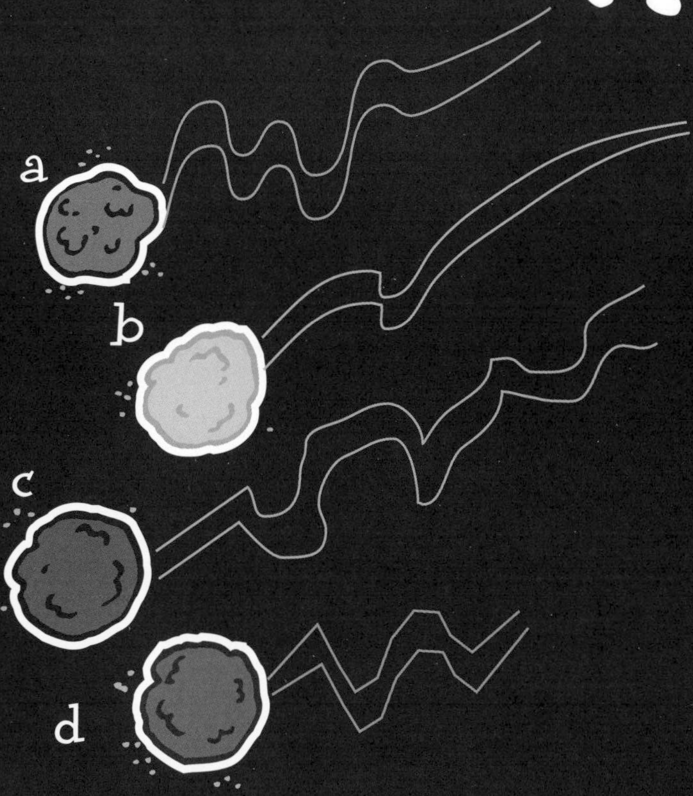

a

b

c

d

What types of boats are these? **142**

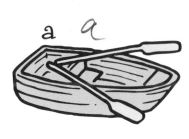
a   a

b

c

d

143

Help the camel through the maze to the oasis.

144

Circle the lowest number.

twenty

14

19

9

ten

22

twelve

11

What does Colonel Buttersnatch's magical mirror say?

Sandcastle building competition today!

Which one doesn't belong?

147

Write the first letter of each picture in the center of the puzzle wheel. You will spell something to do on a rainy day.

148

Divide Farmer Freddy's field into six equal areas.

Which is the missing
piece of the puzzle?

149

a  b  c  d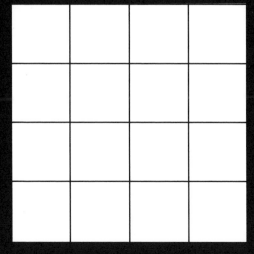

Draw the picture in
the grid, copying
square by square.

150

Can you fill in the missing numbers?

152

Starting with the letter B, cross out every other letter to reveal a small animal.

Starting with the letter Q, cross out every other letter to reveal what's for dinner.

Q C O H L I P C Y K T E R N E S W O N U M P

_____

Chicken Soup

Draw lines to connect the sports equipment.

a

2

1

3

c

b

d

4

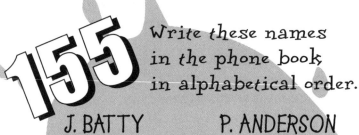

155

Write these names in the phone book in alphabetical order.

J. BATTY   P. ANDERSON
A. THOMPSON   P. ADAMS
D. PETERS   N. PETERS

156

Circle the one that doesn't belong.

King Crusty is examining his jewels. Color the rubies red, the emeralds green, and the sapphires blue.

ruby	sapphire	emerald	ruby
emerald	ruby	sapphire	emerald
ruby	sapphire	emerald	emerald
sapphire	emerald	sapphire	ruby

Follow the lines to see who is calling who.

159

Draw lines to connect the sportspeople with the correct balls.

a

○ 1

b

○ 2

c

⚽ 3

160

Match the clown to his shadow.

a

b

c

d

Which piece
does not belong
to this puzzle? **161**

a

d

e

c

b

h

f

g

Which countries have
these postcards been
sent from? **162**

a

b

c

d

163 Follow the numbers from 1-6 to help the racing car to the finish line.

164 Which things are out of place in the haunted house?

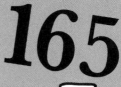

Use the picture clues to fill in the word trail. **166** The last letter of each word is the first letter of the next.

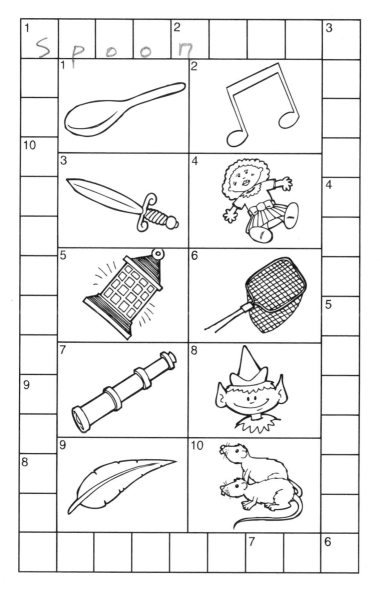

167

Look carefully at the picture. There are six things wrong. Can you find them?

168

Can you fill in the missing numbers?

	−	5	=	13
÷		−		+
2	+		=	
=		=		=
	×	2	=	18

How many dots can
you see on each dice?
How many dots are
there altogether? **169**

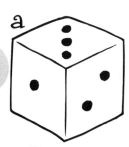

a

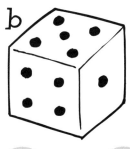

b

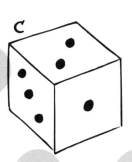

c

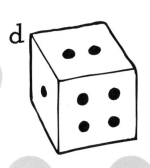

d

Find the letters in
the grid and you will
spell the name of
a country. **170**

	1	2	3	4	5	6
A	C	M	M	S	K	M
B	S	W	R	G	A	O
C	C	B	A	E	M	Q
D	X	H	L	X	T	A
E	P	D	E	G	T	H
F	F	I	J	I	M	H

___ ___ ___ ___ ___ ___
A3 C4 D4 F2 C1 B6

Draw lines to connect the pairs.

a

1

b

2

c

3

Can you find the word PARROT six times in this grid?

N	D	P	A	T	R	S	N	A
P	A	R	R	O	T	T	O	F
R	A	L	D	W	O	P	A	R
W	O	T	N	R	O	A	O	R
R	P	S	P	A	R	R	O	T
D	A	A	D	P	L	R	O	S
T	R	P	A	R	R	O	T	H
K	R	N	B	F	T	T	V	R
D	O	C	P	A	R	R	O	T
A	T	C	G	H	B	H	J	U

Which of these feet belongs to this duck?

a

b

c

d

e

Circle the mistakes in this picture.

175

Who has the most crayons?

a

b

c

d

176

Arrange the beads on this necklace to form a sentence.

I'd   like

visit   to   zoo   the

Help the car through the maze to the rally by spelling something you put in a car.

177

RALLY

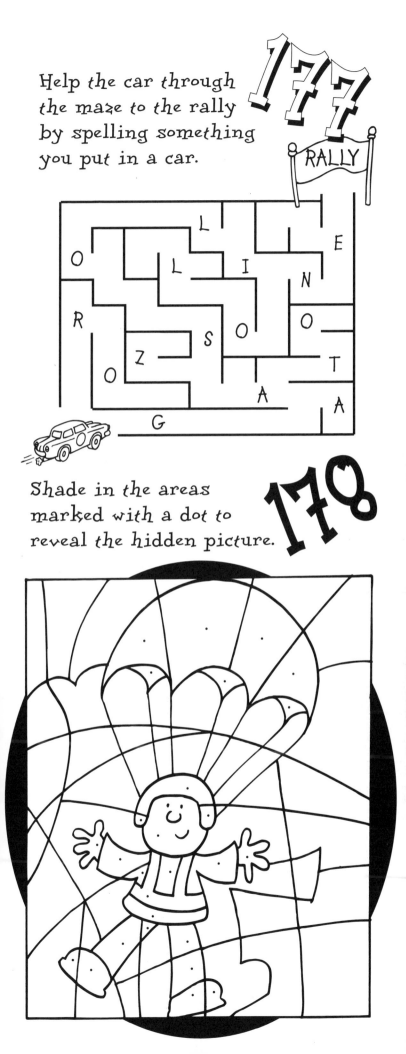

Shade in the areas marked with a dot to reveal the hidden picture.

178

179

Count all the spots on the frogs and write the total number on the lily pad.

180

Follow the lines to find out who's going on which ride.

a   b   c   d

Connect each wizard to a number, then draw that number of stars on each hat.

181

4

6

Draw a line to connect the identical pair of pandas.

182

a

b

c

d

e

183

How many words can you think of that rhyme with "lamp"?

184

Olly the octopus has cold feet! Give him some patterned socks.

Which wheel fits this tractor?

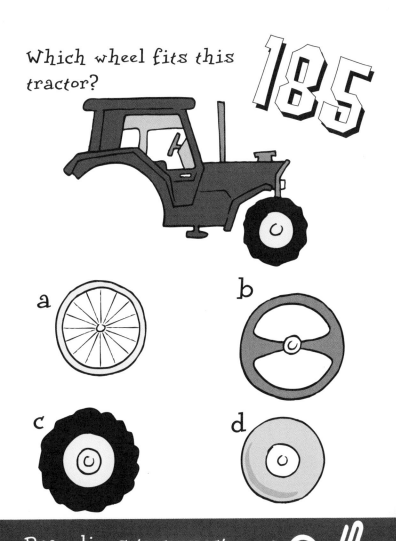

a

b

c

d

Draw lines to connect each animal to its tail.

a

b

c

187 Unscramble the magic word to make the wizard's spell work.

CADARABARAB

188 Starting at number 1, connect the dots to complete the picture.

Unscramble the names of these cities.

LADASL

_____

AWTTAO

_____

IREBLN

_____

Draw lines to connect the matching skylines.

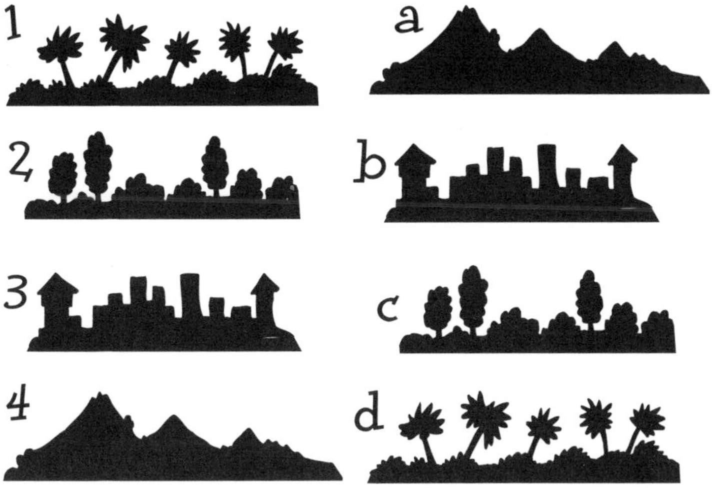

1

a

2

b

3

c

4

d

Unscramble the letters to reveal what is in the magician's hat.

r b
i
a t
b

192 Draw the map in the grid, copying square by square.

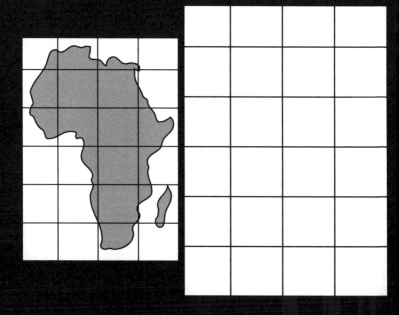

Which is the missing piece of the puzzle?

a

b

c

Draw a face on this pirate.

195

Think of ways to cool this polar bear down. Draw your answers!

196

Find these animals in the word search.

```
I  K  A  N  G  A  R  O  O
S  I  O  D  Z  Y  C  D  L
H  W  J  R  S  O  P  V  M
K  I  T  T  E  N  Z  K  R
G  H  Y  R  I  T  D  E  U
W  F  Y  B  L  Y  S  S  E
K  T  Q  N  K  M  Q  T  K
K  O  A  L  A  F  H  R  Y
I  P  W  R  G  T  U  E  D
D  X  K  O  A  W  P  L  I
```

Draw an animal that lives on dry land and has four legs and a hard shell.

197

Who has the shortest pants?

198

a

b   c

199

Draw circles around the trees that have silly things growing on them!

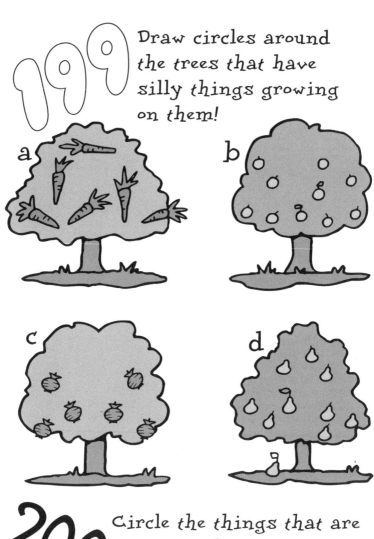

a

b

c

d

200

Circle the things that are wrong in this picture.

Which animals have been mixed up here?

Shade in the areas marked with a dot to reveal the hidden picture.

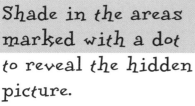

203
In which city would you find the Statue of Liberty?

204
Which two gnomes are exactly the same?

a

b

c

d

e

Can you fill in the missing numbers?

5	−	3	=	2
+	■	÷	■	+
2	×	3	=	6
=	■	=	■	=
7	+	1	=	8

Connect Ben to his shadow.

207

Draw a creature with eight legs that lives in the sea.

208

Can you find the word SQUARE five times in this grid?

P	E	S	Q	U	A	R	E	L	L
W	R	Q	A	G	H	Y	A	K	
S	Q	U	A	R	E	E	N	L	
K	D	A	E	B	P	D	D	S	
S	W	R	L	S	V	T	A	E	
W	T	E	F	Q	B	I	T	P	
D	Q	O	H	U	O	G	U	S	
I	S	Q	U	A	R	E	L	K	
R	M	H	F	R	A	R	B	N	
F	G	T	J	E	F	H	G	Y	

How many words can you *think* of *that* rhyme with "dog"?

Count the heads and legs of these flamingos. What's missing?

211

Write the first letter of each picture clue in the boxes to do the math.

☐ ☐ ☐

+

☐ ☐ ☐

=

☐ ☐ ☐ ☐ ☐ ☐

212

Can you fill in the missing numbers?

3	×		=	12
×		×		×
3	×	2	=	
=		=		=
	×	8	=	72

How many eyes
do spiders have?

213

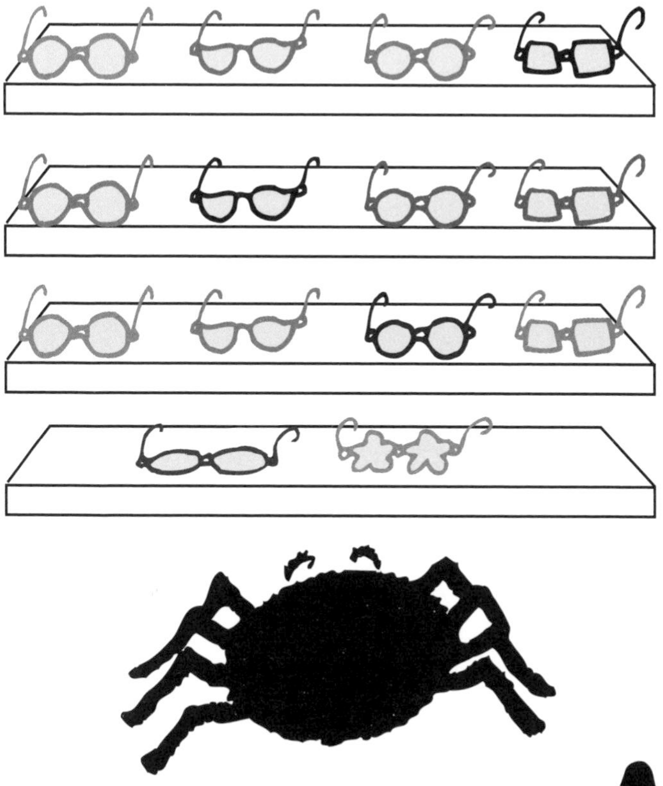

In which country does
the giant panda live
in the wild?

214

INDIA

CHINA

AFRICA

215 What do the stars in the American flag represent?

_____

_____

_____

216 Find six boys' names in the word search.

E	R	F	V	C	P	A	U	Z
R	O	W	T	S	Y	J	F	I
S	B	O	S	T	U	A	R	T
T	E	A	S	E	F	G	E	J
K	R	P	O	V	Q	W	D	H
Y	T	A	L	E	X	L	D	M
S	B	U	C	T	Z	A	I	D
T	G	L	J	K	L	R	E	H

Which ears belong to
which animal? Draw
lines to connect them.

What type of tree has
Gerald the giraffe
eaten?

218

219 Can you spot the differences between these two pictures?

220 How many things beginning with the letter C can you find in this picture?

Connect the vehicles to the correct wheels.

221

Match the rugby player to his shadow.

222

a b c

223 Cross out the letters that appear more than once to reveal where the camel's rider is.

I
P A
D M O
G N R T
P H L E D
B G U R S L

224 Unscramble the letters to reveal what is in the emperor's bowl.

e i
r e

Help the hungry hamsters through the maze to their bag of food.

225

Can you spot the differences between these two pictures?

226

227 What does Derek the detective need to do his job?

228 Fill in the missing numbers.

| 2 | 4 | | 8 |

| 1 | | 3 | 4 |

| 5 | 10 | | 20 |

| 3 | | 9 | 12 |

Draw circles around the animals that hibernate.

a

b

c

d

e

Which of these countries do tigers come from?

INDIA

IRELAND

ITALY

231

Help the waiter through the maze to the customers' table.

232

Beginning with X, cross out every other letter to reveal Mark's favorite subject.

X	H	M	I	P
S	Q	T	R	O
S	R	N	Y	B

_____

Connect each gardener to a number, then draw that number of flowers in each garden.

233

Follow the lines to find out which dog has which bone.

234

a   b   c

b   c   a

1   2   3

235

Find the picture clues in the word search.

E	P	Y	R	A	M	I	D	V
F	I	S	S	Z	U	C	V	G
H	Z	K	P	O	M	I	F	Y
T	Z	E	H	Q	M	S	O	F
G	A	J	I	U	Y	S	X	M
N	B	V	N	X	N	O	T	E
R	F	D	X	T	X	C	B	M
S	P	O	R	T	S	C	A	R
L	K	Q	W	R	T	E	S	A
J	U	G	O	N	D	R	L	A

236

Unscramble the letters on the crocodile's teeth to find out what he likes to eat.

u b a e g r r m h

Draw a straight line
from each problem
to its answer.

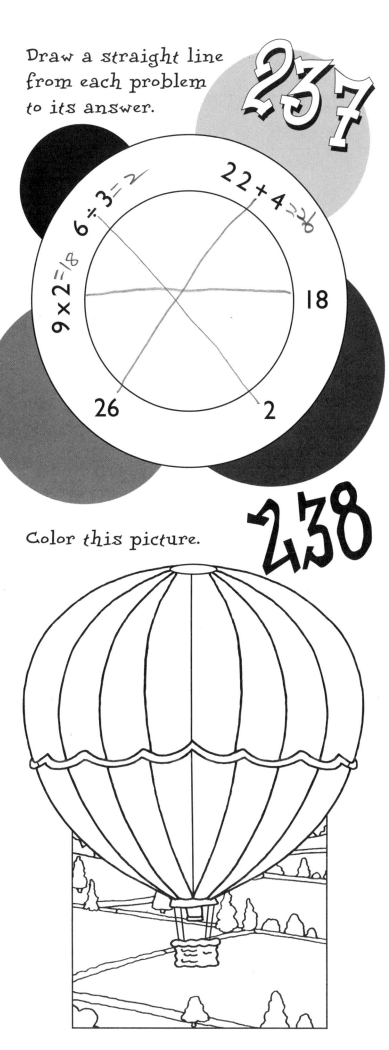

$9 \times 2 = 18$ $6 \div 3 = 2$ $22 + 4 = 26$

18

26   2

Color this picture.

239 How many things beginning with the letter A can you find in this picture?

240 Which is the heaviest item?

Color this picture
using the number key.

1 = red 2 = green 3 = yellow
4 = black 5 = blue

Who has the biggest
allowance?

242

243 Draw yourself on this television screen.

244 Counting by tens, connect the dots to complete the picture.

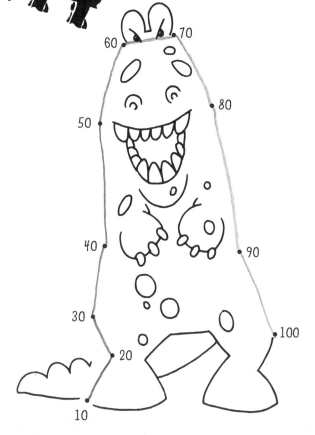

Which animals are usually connected with these things?

245

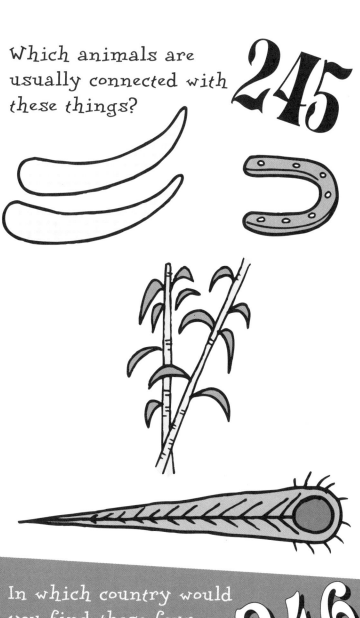

In which country would you find these four animals?

246

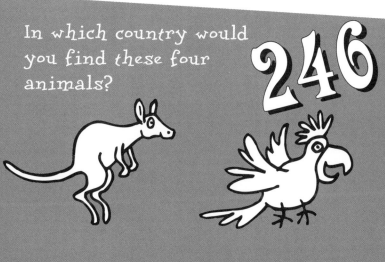

247 Crack this letter code to read the question, then write your answer in the box.

HO WMAN YLE GS DO ESAN OCTO PUSH AVE?

248 Which jar contains the most candy?

a
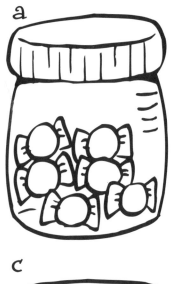

b

c

d

Unscramble the coded message to reveal where the spy needs to leave the secret plans.

What strange thing did Bobby photograph on vacation? Draw the other half.

250

251 Which country is this?

252 What time is it?

Archie Archaeologist
has made a discovery.
Are these things:

253

a) Roman
b) Egyptian
c) Australian?

Use the picture as clues
to find words buried
in the grid.

254

Z	F	H	O	O	K	A	H	P
H	M	G	R	D	S	L	D	I
I	W	O	X	B	D	I	Q	R
S	C	L	B	F	S	B	T	A
F	I	D	T	C	H	E	S	T
J	O	M	A	H	T	Y	G	E
W	R	K	U	R	L	S	D	M
M	A	V	E	R	V	O	C	B
A	E	W	P	A	R	R	O	T
P	Q	U	D	P	E	R	Q	W

255 Use the pictures as clues to complete the crossword.

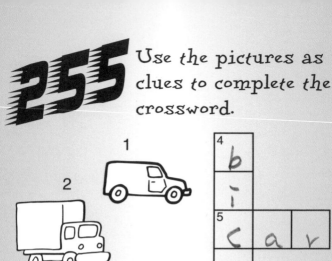

Across:
4. b i c a r (bicycle)
3. a i r p l a n e (airplane)

Down:
1. v
2. t r u c k
4. b i c y c l e
5. c a r

256 How many humps does a dromedary camel have? Draw the camel.

How many cars will be needed to take 20 people to the carvival if each car takes four people?

257

See if you can identify the criminal from the picture.

258

a   b   c   d

259

Can you crack the code to work out this message?

ME ETM
EAT SEV
ENO'
CLO CK.

260

Draw the Stars and Stripes on this flag.

Find the letters in the grid. You will spell a kind of race.

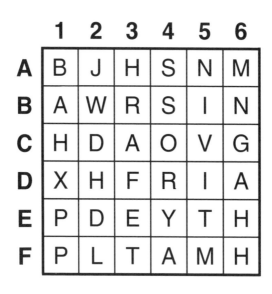

	1	2	3	4	5	6
A	B	J	H	S	N	M
B	A	W	R	S	I	N
C	H	D	A	O	V	G
D	X	H	F	R	I	A
E	P	D	E	Y	T	H
F	P	L	T	A	M	H

___ ___ ___ ___ ___ ___ ___ ___
A6   B1   D4   F4   E5   C1   C4   A5

Each shell is worth one minute. Which crab wins the race?

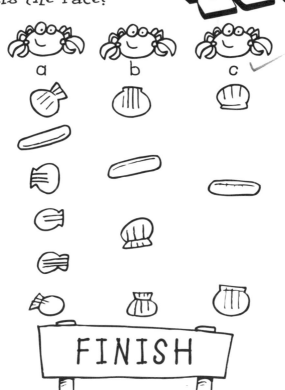

a   b   c

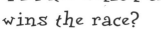

FINISH

263 Rearrange these letters to find out which planet is closest to the sun.

M U C Y E R R

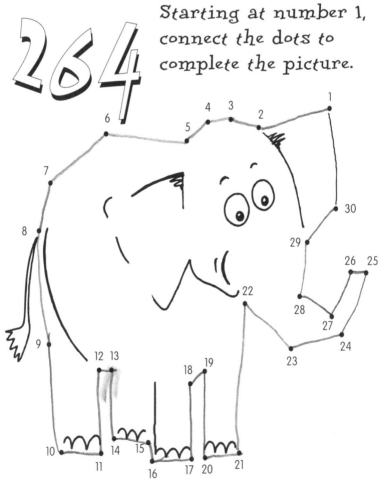

264 Starting at number 1, connect the dots to complete the picture.

How many triangles can you count in this picture?

265

Look carefully at these two pictures. Can you spot the differences between them?

266

The treasure is buried three squares east of the palm tree. Draw an X to mark the spot.

268

Which animal spins a web to catch flies? Draw it in the frame.

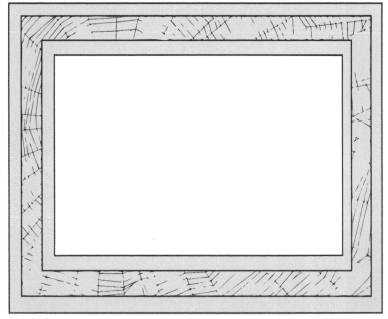

List as many animals as you can that have tails.

_____
_____horse_____
_____
_____
_____
_____snake_____
_____
_____

Help the mice do the math.

269

270

$2+6=8$

$3 \times 4 = 12$

$15-5=10$

271 Color this picture.

272 Help the man through the maze to his boomerang.

Look at the pictures.
Find the words in
the grid.

F	E	U	W	O	D	V	X
L	L	W	A	I	T	E	R
A	E	G	I	V	M	A	O
T	C	U	T	M	E	S	Y
W	H	K	R	O	N	J	E
A	E	B	E	Z	U	A	G
R	F	N	S	L	B	O	M
E	E	I	S	K	F	H	A
Z	C	B	T	Y	U	I	L

Which animal should
not be in the African
jungle?

275

How many worms can you count in William's wormery?

276

Which nation is this?

Which is the capital city of Japan?

a) Osaka
b) Kyoto
c) Tokyo

Unscramble these capital cities.

CRIOA

MORE

NIBOSL

279 Which of these is the lightest?

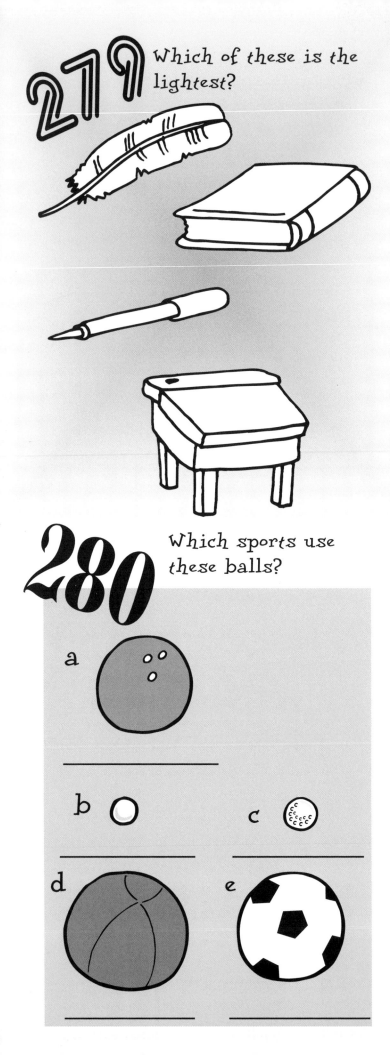

280 Which sports use these balls?

a

_____

b ○   c

_____

d   e

_____   _____

What sport is Martin about to play?

281

Draw features on this face.

282

283

Draw what happens next.

1.

2.

3.

4.

284

Counting up by hundreds, connect the dots.

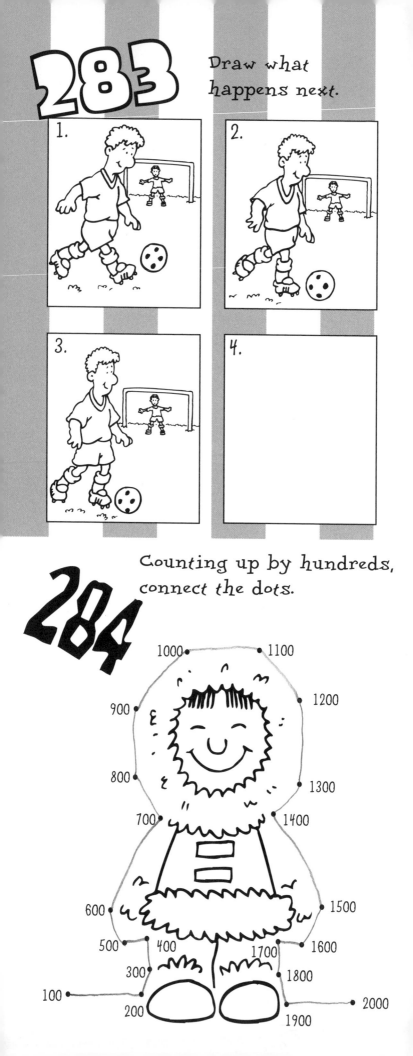

Can you fill in the missing numbers?

285

4	+	2	=	6
×		−		+
2	+	1	=	3
=		=		=
8	+	1	=	9

Name the biggest living bird.

286

287 Draw a line to connect the Viking to his hat.

a

b

c

d

e

288 Which animals have been mixed up here?

I have six letters.
I am a type of mythical creature.
My first is in dawn but not in yawn.
My second is in grow but not in glow.
My third is in sand but not in send.
My fourth is in tiger but not in timer.
My fifth is in toil but not in tail.
My sixth is in nest but not in test.

I am a *dragon*

291

How many circles can you see in this street scene? 16

292

Color this picture.

How many new words
can you make from
"PRETTY POLLY"?

_____

_____

_____

_____

_____

Help the children
through the House
of Horrors maze.

EXIT

295 Cross out the letters that appear twice in the grid. The letters that remain will tell you who left the footprint in the snow.

yeti

A	W	S	Y
E	U	A	H
U	H	T	W
B	I	B	S

296 Draw a circle around the things you would take to school.

Use the pictures as clues to complete the crossword.

297

1. g o l d f i s h
2. m o u s e
3. d o g
4. k i t t e n
5. h o r s e

Cross out the letters that appear twice in the grid. The letters that remain will spell a secret word.

298

DIARY

W	L	D	E	C
I	B	F	P	N
A	N	O	R	L
T	W	C	T	Y
B	E	P	O	F

299 Can you crack the code to work out where the children are meeting?

At the beach

M E ETA TTH EBEA CH

300 Follow the lines to find out which groceries are whose.

a   b   c

1   2   3

Use the picture clues
to fill in the word trail.
The last letter of each
word is the first letter of the next.

301

Check the correct
sentence.

302

☑ Mark drew a picture.

☐ Mark drawed a picture.

303

Circle the things in this picture that begin with the letter P.

304

Which weasel has the smallest bag of popcorn?

a   b   c

Draw the rest of Olly the Octopus's wallpaper, copying square by square.

Draw lines to connect the opposites.

under	day
sharp	over
night	hot
cold	blunt

307 Follow the number-color key to complete this picture.

1 = red   2 = blue   3 = yellow
4 = brown   5 = green

308 Circle the things Handy Harry needs to do his job.

309

Can you unscramble the name of the place where Weird Wilfred comes from?

KAYCW ODOW

_____

_____

310

Start with the letter J and circle every other letter, until you have gone twice around the star in a clockwise direction. You will spell the names of two planets.

311 Look carefully at these two pictures. Can you spot the differences between them?

312 Figure out what the question is and write your answer in the goal.

HOWMA NYPL AYER SI
NASO CC ER TE AM?

Draw hands on this clock to show the time you watch your favorite TV show.

313

Draw lines to label the parts of this computer.

314

mouse	keyboard

monitor

CD-ROM

mouse

keyboard

monitor	CD-ROM

315

Unscramble the words to reveal the foreign destinations.

DEPARTURES

UNILDB

DuBlin

STHENA

ATHens

AVENGE

Geneva

SyDney

YESDNY

316

Can you solve this riddle?

My first is in make but not in take,

My second is in fun but not in fan,

My third is in sand but not in band,

My fourth is in find but not in fond,

My fifth is in clown but not in blown.

What am I?

How many dots,
stars, and stripes
can you see on
these flags?

317

dots = 26   stars = 12

stripes = 15

Look at the glass of ice.
Draw what it will look
like when the ice has
melted.

318

Look at the pictures. Find the words in the grid.

```
T  I  O  R  O  B  I  N  L
W  O  Z  F  R  G  J  B  C
Y  S  W  I  F  T  A  H  Y
L  W  B  Y  A  U  I  P  G
M  A  G  P  I  E  A  I  N
T  N  J  S  P  R  O  P  E
M  E  T  R  Q  E  D  N  T
M  U  F  S  E  I  U  R  H
V  J  G  R  B  P  C  S  G
B  A  X  A  N  Z  K  N  C
```

320

Unscramble the letters to find out what the Alien Eagle has eaten.

CIBCLEY

Bicycle

These pictures are clues to a country. Which country?

Name the planets in our Solar System.

323

Draw a face on this famous picture.

324

Draw lines to connect these animals.

Which octopus has the correct number of legs?

325

What type of spread has been used to make this sandwich? Unscramble the letters to find out. strawberry Jam

326

T S R
B E R
Y A
W R
A J M

Using the clothes key, do the math and write the answers in the boxes.

| hat = 1 | pants = 5 | shoe = 2 |

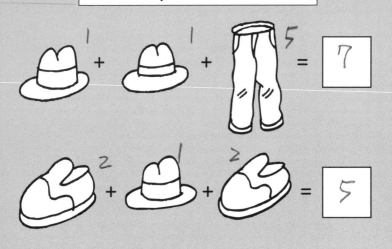

$$\text{hat} + \text{hat} + \text{pants} = 7$$

$$\text{shoe} + \text{hat} + \text{shoe} = 5$$

Draw a head on this sea monster and make it as scary as you can!

Mildred the monster is looking in her magic mirror. Draw what she sees.

Color the hot things red and the cold things blue.

331 How many stars can you count?

332 Look in the word search for the objects below. Circle the words.

```
L E C L O C K O
A I U Z B E H A
B P R D O L I N
R K T R V C F T
O L A M P J B I
N U I T D G O F
Q O N L H T O Y
W E S P D I K S
O I L K J W Q V
```

Point the compass arrow in a south-westerly direction.

333

What is a Tasmanian devil?

334

a) a real animal
b) a legend
c) a naughty Tasmanian child

335

How many four-letter words can you make from the word "RHINOCEROS"?

336

Do the math and write the answers in the crossword grid.

1. 15 ÷ 3 = 5
2. 5 - 5 = 0
3. 14 ÷ 2 = 7
4. 7 + 4 = 11
5. 3 x 3 = 9

1 five
2 zero
3 seven
4 eleven
5 nine

Starting with the letter "a", follow the alphabet to connect the dots and complete the picture.

337

Can you see the mistake in this picture?

338

339 Shade in *the* areas marked with a dot to reveal *the* hidden picture.

340 Draw what you think happens next.

Draw what you ate for dinner last night.

Write the first letter of each picture in the center of the puzzle wheel. Unscramble the letters to spell a word.

343

Can you solve this riddle?

Our first is in mat but not in sat,

Our second is in did but not in dad,

Our third is in cat but not in bat,

Our last is in bed but not in bad.

What are we?

Mice

344

Use the pictures as clues to complete the crossword.

		¹S	
²S	a	n	d
		a	
⁴o		k	
³c	a	m	e	l
s			
⁵p	y	r	a	m	i	d
s			

Do you know what type of dinosaur this is?

345

_____

Draw lines from the problems to the answers.

346

5 + 5 = 10

6 + 4 = 10

7 + 3 = 10

2 × 5 = 10

10 ÷ 1 = 10

10

347

Which countries are these the capital cities of?

VIENNA

Austria

DUBLIN

Ireland

LISBON

Portugal

PARIS

France

348

Each pair of goggles adds one minute. Who wins the race?

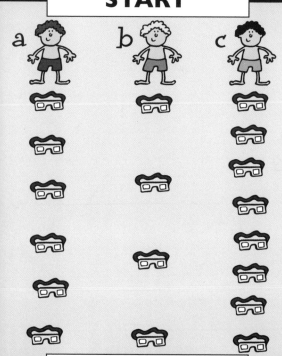

Starting at number 1, connect the dots to complete the picture.

Cross out the letters that appear twice in the grid. The letters that remain spell a part of the body.

O	D	A	V	S
S	L	I	M	N
M	P	D	Q	A
I	Q	C	E	O
C	G	N	V	P

351

Draw the picture in the grid, copying square by square.

352

Think of words that end with "th". Write them on the tub.

Can you fill in the missing numbers?

353

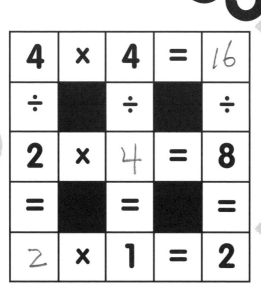

4	**×**	**4**	**=**	16
÷		**÷**		**÷**
2	**×**	4	**=**	**8**
=		**=**		**=**
2	**×**	**1**	**=**	**2**

Draw features on these two heads.

354

355

Help Dave through the number grid to the beach sign. He can move in any direction one square at a time, but can only cross even-numbered squares.

BEACH >

3	9	15	21	19	31	36	13	27
7	12	50	8	3	1	12	29	33
9	32	29	16	28	11	6	5	51
31	26	5	1	34	3	20	9	49
9	4	2	61	40	4	10	33	37
13	59	8	19	27	3	51	1	9
61	3	14	53	1	47	23	7	9
2	6	10	21	3	51	39	63	7

356

How many spots does Sindy have?
How many stripes does Sandy have?

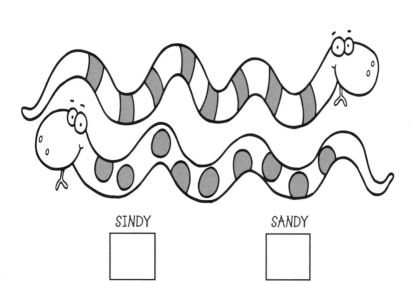

SINDY

SANDY

How many differences can you spot between Simon and his shadow?

Do the math and find the answers in the word search grid.

$24 \div 8 = 3$ ✓ $15 \div 3 = 5$ ✓ $6 + 8 = 14$ ✓

$6 \times 2 = 12$ ✓ $10 \times 3 = 30$ ✓ $22 - 3 = 19$ ✓

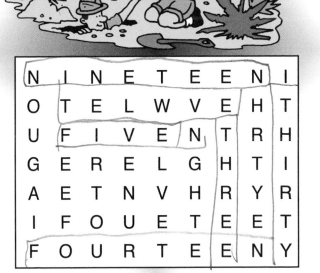

N	I	N	E	T	E	E	N	I
O	T	E	L	W	V	E	H	T
U	F	I	V	E	N	T	R	H
G	E	R	E	L	G	H	T	I
A	E	T	N	V	H	R	Y	R
I	F	O	U	E	T	E	E	T
F	O	U	R	T	E	E	N	Y

359 It costs 20¢ to ride the school bus. If the driver has taken $2.00, how many children are on the bus? Draw them.

SCHOOL BUS

360 Draw lines to match each dish to the country it originates from.

curry — Japan

sushi — Hungary

goulash — India

Cross out the letters that appear twice in the grid. The letters that remain will spell a boy's name.

D	J	I	Z	W
T	G	U	Q	A
M	Q	O	E	H
H	O	G	D	T
I	W	Z	S	U

Imagine you have been on vacation on Mars. Draw a picture of your new Martian friend.

363 How many weeks are there in a year?

Mon	Tue	Wed	Thur	Fri	Sat	Sun
						7
			4	5	6	14
1	2	3	11	12	13	21
8	9	10	18	19	20	28
15	16	17	25	26	27	
22	23	24				
29	30	31				

364 Look at Kurt's photographs. Which city did he visit?

How many new words can you make from "Planet Earth"?

ANSWERS

1. A.
2. Stethoscope.
3. Walrus.
4. Pisa, Italy.
5. a-h; b-g; c-f; d-e.
6. Strings.
9. C.

10.
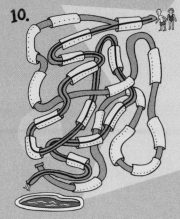

13. C.

14.

15.

S	N	E	A	K	E	R	S
J	D	I	N	Z	P	W	O
W	L	O	F	U	N	K	C
F	I	B	Y	T	C	A	K
W	O	L	J	E	A	N	S
E	N	J	K	L	P	R	T
K	N	U	Y	V	G	I	O
C	S	H	I	R	T	E	B
K	L	R	V	O	P	J	G

17. Walrus.

18.

20. 5 circles;
2 *triangles*;
2 squares.

21. 6 + 3 = 9;
2 + 2 = 4;
5 + 9 = 9.

23. 1-igloo; 2-teepee;
3-tree house.

24. The mountain.

25. 1 - suitcase;
2 - egg; 3 - girl;
4 - lightbulb;
5 - balloons;
6 - socks;
7 - starfish;
8 - hands.

26. 9.55; 8.40; 2.30.

27. cow-bow-bog-
bug-rug.

28. Piece d.

29. Child b.

30.

31. The star with
six points.

32. Alligator;
armadillo; butterfly;
crocodile; iguana;
lizard; pangolin;
snake. Did you
think of more?

33.

34. Tree; motorcycle.

35. Rolling pin.

36. Wrench.

37. Roadrunner c.

38. Flying pig c.

39. 11 squares.

40. Bamboo.

42. Blue whale.

43. A - C.

44. A - crocus;
b - oak tree;
c - apple tree;
d - daffodil;
e - daisy;
f - palm tree.

45. 23 bubbles.

46. 10 coconuts.

48.

50.

51. 16 sides.

54. Seven ghosts.

56. Football.

58. 4; 8; 12; 16.
10; 20; 30; 40.
20; 40; 60.

59.

Q	W	C	H	U	R	C	H	L
T	J	B	O	D	V	D	X	I
O	S	Z	U	A	F	B	J	G
W	C	P	S	K	J	A	R	H
E	H	V	E	S	E	R	C	T
R	O	X	R	B	H	N	T	H
C	O	T	T	A	G	E	O	O
J	L	A	M	L	H	T	D	U
D	K	T	V	V	N	U	G	S
W	L	R	C	A	S	T	L	E

60. 10 pieces.

62.

63.

65. 3.00; 9.15; 1.30.

66. Rabbit, giraffe, duck, and pig.

67. A - gardener;
B - teacher;
C - doctor.

68. Smell, taste, touch, sight, and sound.

70. August.

71. 16 spots.

72.

73. HOUSTON DYNAMO.

74. 35 books.

75. A - F.

77. 15 minutes;
20 minutes;
10 minutes;
30 minutes.

78. 27; 45.
4; 12; 16; 24.
25; 15; 10.

79. PEACH.

80.

82.

Y	H	U	I	O	P	B	L
S	A	F	G	H	J	U	K
R	C	M	O	U	S	E	S
C	A	S	O	L	H	J	G	A
A	T	V	B	N	M	I	C
E	E	C	A	F	Y	E	H
E	R	A	B	B	I	T	Y
G	O	L	D	F	I	S	H
D	O	G	E	O	H	A	M

83. Chicago Fire;
New York Red
Bulls; LA Galaxy;
Philadelphia Union.

84. Antarctic.

85. 10 units; 8 units;
7 units.

86. A-5, B-3; C-4;
D-2; E-1.

87.

6	−	1	=	5
+		×		×
2	×	1	=	2
=		=		=
8	−	1	=	7

88. Girl b.

89. A - 7 odd;
B - 4 even; C - 3 odd;
D - 6 even.

90. WIZARD.

91.

Crossword:
- 2 (down) SAILING
- 1 (across) CYCLING
- 3 (across) JAVELIN
- 4 (across) GOLF

92. A and D.

93. Castle.

94.

Crossword:
- 1 (down) SAILBOAT
- 1 (across) SHIP
- 2 (across) DINGHY
- 3 (across) ROWBOAT

96. B - dinosaur.

97. Runner.

98.

100. EIFFEL TOWER

101. 12 buttons.

102. BUFFALO.

103. A-4; B-4; C-6; D-7; E-4; F-4. Oldcastle.

104. Candy bar and watch.

105. Thomas.

107. Ice hockey.

108.

109. Snake; parrot; lion; zebra.

110. C and H.

112.

2 × 2
9 + 3
8
15
4
3
2 × 4
10 + 5

113. CAT.

114. PET; LOG; RED.

115. PARIS; LONDON; LOS ANGELES; SYDNEY.

117.

Word search: MERCURY, SATURN, VENUS, MARS, EARTH

118. Mirror.

120. A-3; B-4; C-2; D-1.

121.

Crossword:
- 1 (down) KANGAROO
- 2 (across) RABBIT
- 4 (down) FROG
- 4 (across) FLEA
- 3 (across) GRASSHOPPER

122. Breakfast; handsome; earring; bluebell; seahorse.

123.

125. HENRY.

128.

129. THE PLANS ARE HIDDEN.

130. A train.

131. The dinosaur.

134. LEMON.

135. 10 floors.

136. a) 5+4=9
b) 5+5=10
c) 6+5=11

137. The gerbil.

138. 4 + 4 - 2 = 6;
3 + 2 + 4 = 9.

140. Pirate d.

141. Comet c.

142. A - row boat;
B - sailboat;
C - tugboat;
D - motorboat.

143.

144. 9.

145. Sandcastle building competition today!

146. The igloo.

147. Puzzle.

149. Piece d.

151.

3	×	2	=	6
+		−		−
1	×	1	=	1
=		=		=
4	+	1	=	5

152. HAMSTER.

153. CHICKEN SOUP.

154. A-3; B-4; C-1; D-2.

155. Adams, P.; Anderson P.; Batty, J.; Peters, D.; Peters, N.; Thompson, A..

156. The eagle.

158. A-2; B-3; C-1.

159. A-3; B-2; C-1.

160. Shadow b.

161. Piece b.

162. A-Mexico; B-Scotland; C-France; D-Australia.

163.

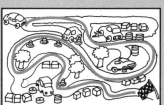

164.

166. 1 spoon; 2 notes; 3 sword; 4 doll; 5 lantern; 6 net; 7 telescope; 8 elf; 9 feather; 10 rats.

167.

168.

18	−	5	=	13
÷		−		+
2	+	3	=	5
=		=		=
9	×	2	=	18

169. A-6; B-10; C-6; D-7. Total = 29.

170. MEXICO.

171. A-3; B-1; C-2.

172.

```
N D P A T R S N A
P A R R O T T O F
R A L D W O P A R
W O T N R O A O R
R P S P A R R O T
D A A D P L R O S
T R P A R R O T H
K R N B F T T V R
D O C P A R R O T
A T C G H B H J U
```

173. Picture c.

174.

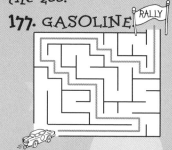

175. Lion cub a.

176. I'd like to visit the zoo.

177. GASOLINE

179. 16 spots.

180. A - pirate ship; B - roller coaster; C - slide; D - big wheel.

182. B and d.

185. Wheel c.

186. Pig-b; horse-c; rabbit-a.

187. ABRACADABRA.

189. DALLAS; OTTAWA; BERLIN.

190. 1-d; 2-c; 3-b; 4-a.

191. Rabbit.

193. Piece c.

196.

```
I K A N G A R O O
S I O D Z Y C D L
H W J R S O P V M
K I T T E N Z K R
G H Y R I T D E U
W F Y B L Y S S E
K T Q N K M Q T K
K O A L A F H R Y
I P W R G T U E D
D X K O A W P L I
```

198. Boy b.

199. Trees a and c.

200.

201. Ostrich, rabbit, elephant, and horse.

203. New York.

204. B and d.

205.

5	−	3	=	2
+		÷		+
2	×	3	=	6
=		=		=
7	+	1	=	8

206. Shadow d.

208.

```
P E S Q U A R E L
W R Q A G H Y A K
S Q U A R E E N L
K D A E B P D D S
S W R L S V T A E
W T E F Q B I T P
D Q O H U O G U S
I S Q U A R E L K
R M H F R A R B N
F G T J E F H G Y
```

210. A pair of legs.

211. Ten + two = twelve.

212.

3	×	4	=	12
×		×		×
3	×	2	=	6
=		=		=
9	+	8	=	72

213. 8 eyes.

214. CHINA.

215. The states of the Union.

216.

218. Palm tree.

219.

220. Cup, car, coat, clock, caterpillar, case, cards, cat, cloak, clouds, cow, child.

221.

222. Shadow a.

223. I AM ON THE BUS.

224. Rice.

226.

227. Derek needs the magnifying glass.

228. 2, 4, <u>6</u>, 8;
1, <u>2</u>, 3, 4;
5, 10, <u>15</u>, 20;
3, <u>6</u>, 9, 12.

229. d.

230. INDIA.

232. HISTORY.

234. A-3; B-1; C-2.

235.

236. Hamburger.

237.

6÷3   22+4
9×2   18
26   2

239. Abacus; astronaut; ax; ambulance; asteroid; awning; antenna; apple; alien.

240. Wheelbarrow.

242. Child a.

245. Tusks – elephant; horseshoe – horse; bamboo – panda; feather – peacock.

246. Australia.

247. How many legs does an octopus have? 8

248. Jar c.

249. MAILBOX.

250. A cow wearing a hat.

251. France.

252. 9.00; 11.15; 7.00; 3.00.

253. A- Roman.

254.

Z	F	H	O	O	K	A	H	P	
H	M	G	R	D	S	L	D	I	
I	W	O	X	B	D	I	Q	R	
S	C	L	B	F	S	B	T	A	
F	I	D	T	C	H	E	S	T	
J	O	M	A	H	T	Y	G	E	
W	R	K	U	R	L	S	D	M	
M	A	V	E	R	V	O	C	B	
A	E	W	P	A	R	R	O	T	
P	Q	U	D	P	E	R	Q	W	

255.

```
        B
        I
      C A R
        Y
  V   T C
  A I R P L A N E
  N   U
      C
      K
```

256. A dromedary camel has one hump.

257. Five cars.

258. Person a.

259. MEET ME AT SEVEN O'CLOCK.

261. MARATHON.

262. Crab c wins.

263. MERCURY.

265. 15 triangles.

266.

267.

270. 2 + 6 = 8;

3 × 4 = 12;

15 – 5 = 10.

272.

273.

F	E	U	W	O	D	V	X	
L	L	W	A	I	T	E	R	
A	E	G	I	V	M	A	O	
T	C	U	T	M	E	S	Y	
W	H	K	R	O	Z	J	E	
A	R	B	E	Z	U	A	G	
R	F	N	S	L	B	O	M	
E	E	I	S	K	F	H	A	
Z	C	B	T	Y	U	I	L	

274. Giant panda.

275. Nine worms.

276. United Kingdom.

277. C - Tokyo.

278. CAIRO; ROME; LISBON.

279. The feather is the lightest.

280. A - bowling;

B - badminton;

C - golf;

D - basketball;

E - soccer.

281. Badminton.

285.

4	+	2	=	6
×		−		+
2	+	1	=	3
=		=		=
8	+	1	=	9

286. Ostrich.

287. D - the helmet.

288. Mouse, elephant, ostrich, and lion.

289. Dragon.

290.

291. 16 circles.

294.

295. YETI.

296. Calculator, schoolbag, pencil, ruler.

297.

```
    G
 ²M O U S E
    L
   ³D O G
    F
 ⁴K I T T E N
    S
   ⁵H O R S E
```

298. DIARY.

299. AT THE BEACH.

300. A-2; B-1; C-3.

301. 1. Pumpkin;
2. nest; 3. teapot;
4. tuba; 5. angel;
6. lemon; 7. nail;
8. ladder; 9. robot;
10. turnip.

302. Mark drew a picture.

303. Pictures; palm trees; plane; photos; photo booth; pilot; passport; plant; pot.

304. Weasel a.

306. Under - over; sharp - blunt; night - day; cold - hot.

308. Trowel and bricks.

309. WACKY WOOD.

310. JUPITER and MERCURY.

311.

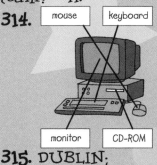

312. How many players in a soccer team? - 11.

314.

mouse · keyboard · monitor · CD-ROM

315. DUBLIN; ATHENS; GENEVA; SYDNEY.

316. Music.

317. 26 dots; 12 stars; 15 stripes.

319.

```
T I O R O B I N L
W O 3 F R G j B C
Y S W I F T A H Y
L W B Y A U I P G
M A G P I E A I N
T N J S P R O P E
M E T R Q E   N T
M U F S E I U R H
V J G R B P C S G
B A X A N 3 K N C
```

320. BICYCLE.

321. Spain.

322. Mercury; Venus; Earth; Mars; Jupiter; Saturn; Uranus; Neptune.

325. Octopus b.

326. Strawberry jam.

327. 1 + 1 + 5 = 7; 2 + 1 + 2 = 5.

331. 21 stars.

332.

L	E	C	L	O	C	K	O	
A	I	U	Z	B	E	H	A	
B	P	R	D	O	L	I	N	
R	K	T	R	V	C	F	T	
O	L	A	M	P	J	B	I	
N	U	I	T	D	G	O	F	
Q	O	N	L	H	T	O	Y	
W	E	S	P	D	I	K	S	
O	I	L	K	J	W	Q	V	

333.

334. A - real animal.

336.

```
            ¹F
            I
  ²Z  ³S    V
  ⁴E  L  E  V  E  N
  R   V
  O   E
            ⁵N  I  N  E
```

338. Boat in field.

342. Rocket.

343. Mice.

344.

```
            ¹S
      ²S A  N  D
            A
      ⁴O    K
      ³C A  M  E  L
      A     S
⁵P Y R A  M  I  D
      I     S
      S
```

345. Stegosaurus.

346.

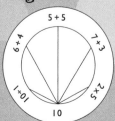

347. Austria; Ireland; Portugal; France.

348. Swimmer b.

350. LEG.

353.

4	×	4	=	16
÷		÷		÷
2	×	4	=	8
=		=		=
2	×	1	=	2

355.

BEACH

3	9	15	21	19	31	36	13	27
7	12	50	8	3	1	12	29	33
9	32	29	16	28	11	6	5	51
31	26	5	1	34	3	20	9	49
9	4	2	61	40	4	10	33	37
13	59	6	19	27	3	51	1	9
61	3	14	53	1	47	23	7	9
2	6	10	21	3	51	39	63	7

356. Sindy has 9 stripes; Sandy has 8 spots.

357.

358.

N	I	N	E	T	E	E	N	I
O	T	E	L	W	V	E	H	T
U	F	I	V	E	N	T	R	H
G	E	R	E	L	G	H	T	Y
A	E	T	N	V	H	R	Y	R
I	F	O	U	E	T	E	E	T
F	O	U	R	T	E	E	N	Y

359. 10 children.

360. Curry - India; sushi - Japan; goulash - Hungary.

361. JAMES.

363. 52 weeks in a year.

364. London.